EVOLUTION OF ISLAM IN AMERICA

MASHA BOOKS

Compiled and Written:

Jason Luke Starr

Reference Source:

Britannica

Study.com

Metropolitan Museum of Art

Qatr.us

Image courtesy:

Inspirock

Alamy

iStock

Getty images

Layout and Design: NextStage Events and Communication

First Published: 2018

Introduction

Everyone knows the famous story about Christopher Columbus and his voyage to India was one meant to find a new trade route. This voyage was due to Christopher Colombus wanting to capitalize on the spice trade between Europe and Asia. The journey however, ended with him discovering a new land, that many years later came to be known as the Land of Freedom and Opportunity.

But what many don't know is that the continent of America was visited, not by the Italians but by another Civilization many years ago.

While the rest of the world was busy getting its footing, understanding the world around them; another civilization had established themselves in many parts of the known world. For a long period of time the Muslim civilization spread to most of the world and became the most advanced civilization of the time. They invented and introduced concepts and ideas that are still in use today, as well as travelled to many parts of the world, spreading their knowledge wherever they went.

So much so, that when the civilization began to decline, many countries and its people still continued to follow Islam. While the Muslim Empire came to an end, another was taking centre stage. At this time, many people from European countries made the migration to America, with the aim of starting a new life and becoming rich. They brought with them their hopes, dreams, ideas, thoughts, views and their religions.

While many of the early Americans were either Catholics or Protestants, there was also a small group of people who practiced Islam in secret. This book will attempt to chronicle the Evolution of Islam, from when it first landed on the shores of the newly founded continent to what it has become now, gaining prominence due to certain famous members that it influenced along the way.

Contents

THE LAST CAMP OF
HI JOLLY
BORN SOMEWHERE IN SYRIA
ABOUT 1828
DIED AT QUARTZSITE
DECEMBER 16 1902
CAME TO THIS COUNTRY

THE MOTHER MOSQUE OF AMERICA
ISLAMIC CULTURAL
&
HERITAGE CENTER

Initial Stages

For many years, Islam was a religion that remained primarily in central countries like Egypt, Persia, Turkey, Saudi Arabia etc. It did spread to the west, but was limited only to Cordoba in Spain. It did not spread to the newly discovered continent of North America for many years. This leads to the question, How did it start?

1178 CE

While many have attributed Columbus with the discovery of North America, truth was, the Muslim world already knew about the continent. This is backed up by the Sung Document which records a number of Muslim sailors who travelled to a land called Mu-Lan-Pi (otherwise known as the American continent). The document is also mentioned in a publication called The Khotan Amirs 1933. The journey to the continent took place in 1178 CE, many years before the famous Zheng He travelled the seas.

Zheng He was a famous Chinese explorer, fleet admiral and mariner from the Ming Dynasty

1300 CE

More than a century later, Abu Bakri or Abu Bakr II, who ruled Mali in West Africa started a series of sea voyages to North America in the early 1300s. It was during this time, the Mandingo Muslims from Mali and other parts of West Africa were said to have arrived in the Gulf of Mexico, then travelled up the Mississippi River to explore the interior portion of the newly discovered continent.

Many years after these expeditions, Columbus made his legendary discovery. After this, a great many people from the east migrated to the new continent. Along with them came the slaves they had under their employ, to help build and construct towns and cities for the settlers.

Artistic rendition of Abu Bakr II

1513 CE

Piri Reis finishes the first World Map. Through the research and information gained from other maps, Piri Reis also includes America on the map. The artistry of the map is greater than any others that came before, it and was well received by all.

First World Map drawn by Piri Reis

Piri Reis, a famous navigator and cartographer

1530 CE

During the following three centuries of slave trade, more than 10 million Africans were torn from their homes and brought to the shores of Cuba, Mexico and North America. Most of the slaves came from West Africa and were known as Fulas, Fula Jallon, Fula Toro and Massina.

Slave Trade

Shipping slaves

Many researchers believe that at least 10-50 percent of these slaves were Muslims but were prevented from practicing religion. There are historical records, indicating that many enslaved Muslims prayed in Arabic and some even composed literature and commentaries on the Quran.

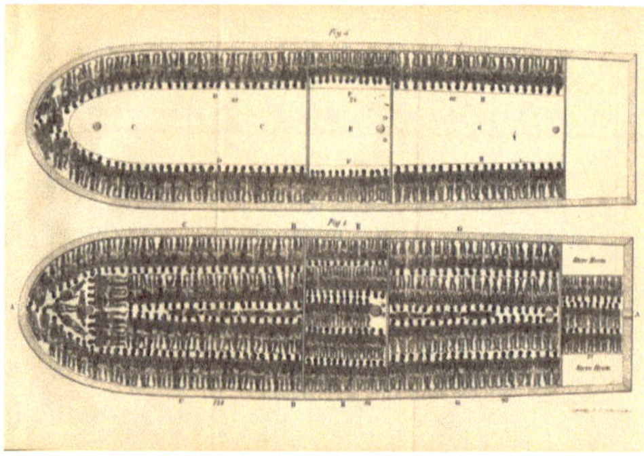

Slaves being transported by ships were tightly packed

As time rolled on, some Muslim slaves were given a private praying area by their owner. Ayuba Suleiman Diallo was one notable slave who regularly faced opposition when attempting to perform his religious duties. It was through sheer persistence alone that his master eventually allotted him a private location for prayer.

Ayuba Suleiman Diallo was a famous American Muslim and victim of the Atlastin slave trade. His memoirs are published as one of the earliest first person account of the slave trade.

1539 CE

Among the many slaves, there was one man, known in the records as Estevanico Mustafa Zemmouri, better known as Estevanico. He was one of the first documented native African man to reach the United States. Estevanico was enslaved as a youth by the Portuguese and served with Panfilo de Narvaez in 1527 on his expedition ship. The ship sank, due to unfavourable weather conditions.

Ship used by Panfilo de Navarez

Most of the crew on the ship died at sea

He was one of four other survivors who landed at what is now called Galveston, Texas and later travelled Southwest America before reaching Mexico City. Historical records from the 1700s would reveal that the Spanish 'Moors' who lived in South Carolina were mostly composed of people expelled from their homeland.

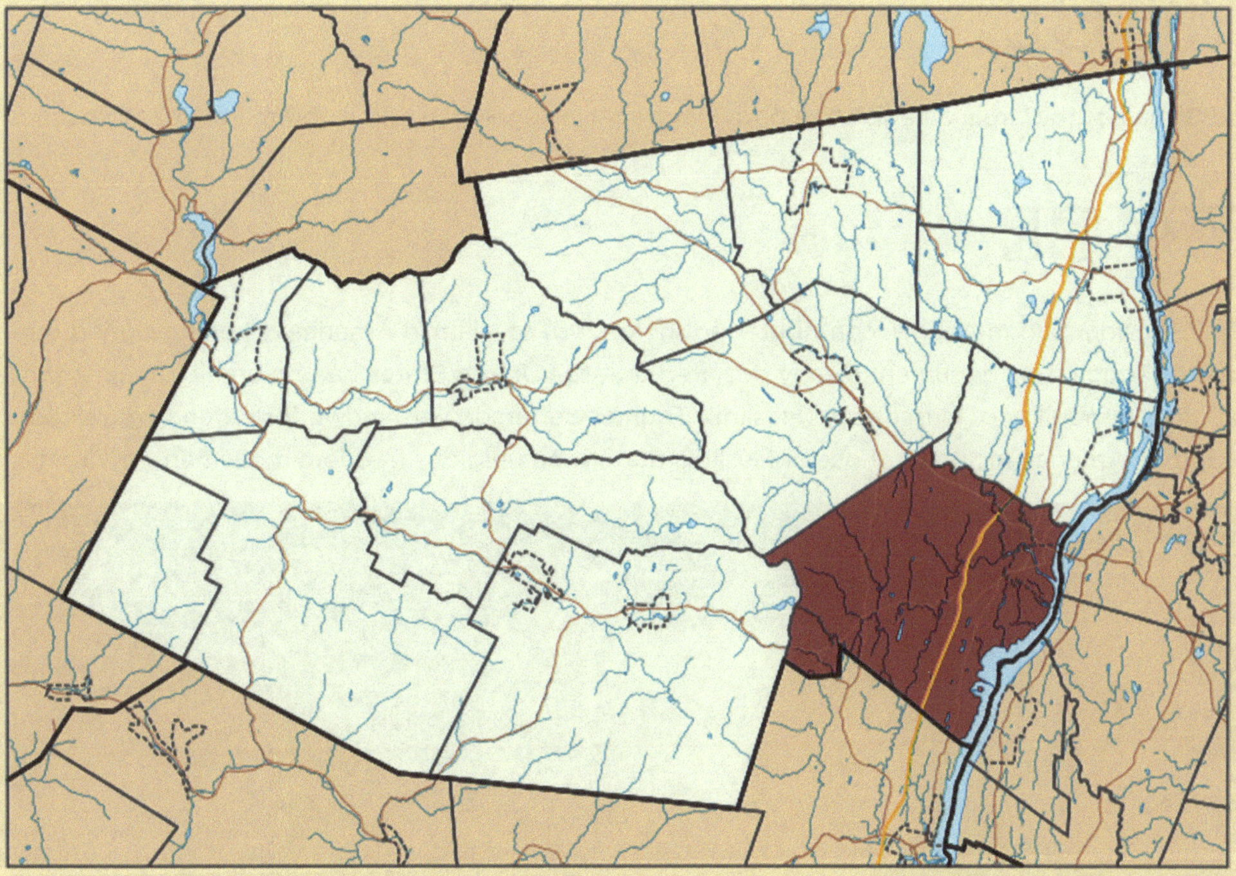

Another account of a possible Muslim immigrant was an Egyptian by the name of 'Norsereddin'. The account comes from Dutch settlers of the Catskill Mountains and they talk about how Norsereddin settled in the vicinity of the Catskill mountain house, where he befriended the local indigenous American chief, Shandaken. Islam was not very prevalent at the time and most Muslims would pray in secret.

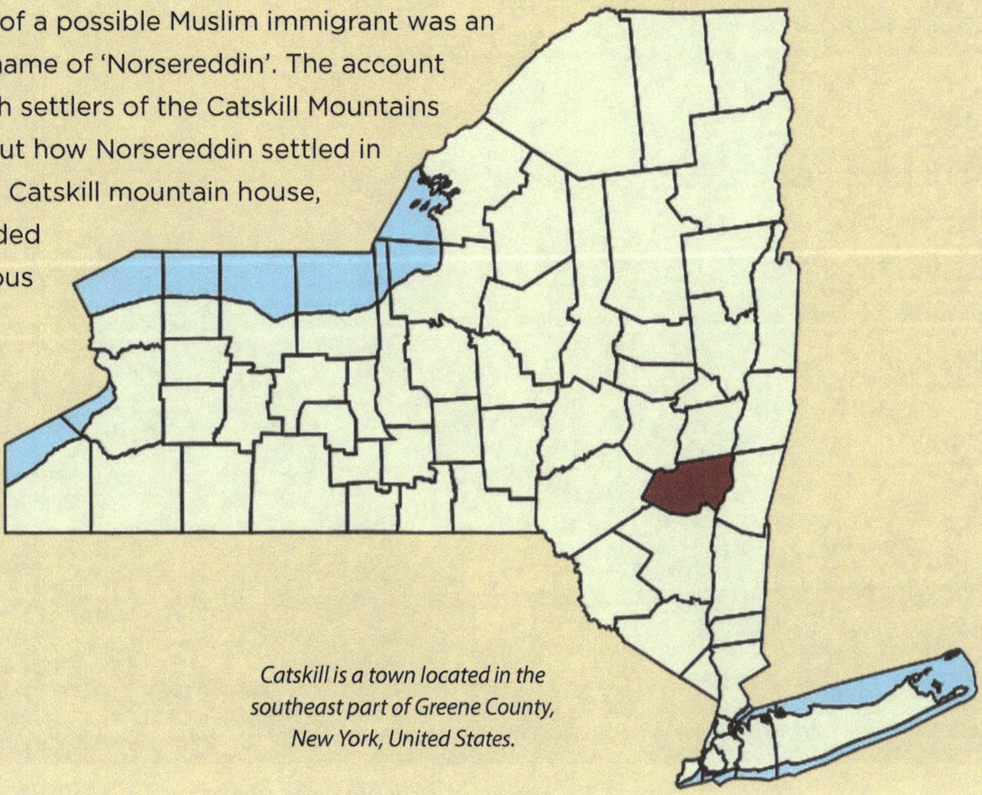

Catskill is a town located in the southeast part of Greene County, New York, United States.

1790 CE

In 1790 the South Carolina Legislative body gave special legal status to a community of Moroccans.

1797 CE

In 1797 President John Adams, contributed to the growth of Islam in America, when he signed the Treaty of Tripoli. This document clearly declared that the United States had no enmity against the laws, religion or tranquility of Mussulmen (Muslim). Thomas Jefferson was known for defending religious freedom in America including those of Muslims during the religious freedom movement in Virginia.

2nd President of the United States, John Adams

1807 CE

Omar Ibn Said is well known for a series of books on History and Theology

Later, Omar Ibn Said was brought to Charleston South Carolina in 1807 as a slave. He eventually ran away, as he could not bear living as a slave, but was caught and imprisoned in North Carolina. During his confinement he wrote in an unreadable script and spoke in an unfamiliar language to those around him, causing everyone to brand him a lunatic. It was thanks to Governor John Owen, who bought him and gave him minimal work that Omar Ibn Said narrowly avoided hanging. Omar was later granted a house on the Owen estate and the Governor treated him less like a slave and more like a friend of the family. Said later wrote an autobiography and maintained contact with other Muslims in the immediate area. Though he converted to Christianity in 1820, there are many who believe that Omar still practiced Islam, based on dedications to Prophet Muhammad written in the Arabic translation of his Bible.

Masjid Omar Ibn Said found in Fayetteville, North Carolina

When Muslims were still slaves, they used their literacy to leverage their freedom through their labour. Slave owners knew about this and would exploit their slaves' proficiencies in certain disciplines and their knowledge in professional backgrounds. Some Muslims had jobs like personal servants, book-keepers and coachmen. This allowed them to gain physical mobility and access information that was normally shared within the white society.

1807 CE

Yarrow Mamout, a notable name from Georgetown, Washington D.C was a versatile man in his day. Mamout was a jack of all trades and he used this skill during his service to the Beall family to make charcoal, work on the Maryland ship, make bricks and weave baskets. His eventual brick-making agreement with Beall's wife would have lead to his manumission (freeing of slave) in April 1807. Instead of returning to his homeland however, Mamout chose to remain in the U.S and became a shareholder in the Columbia Bank. At present, there are portraits of Mamout hung in the Historical Society of Pennsylvania and the Georgetown Public library in Washington.

Philadelphia Museum of Art

Georgetown Public Library

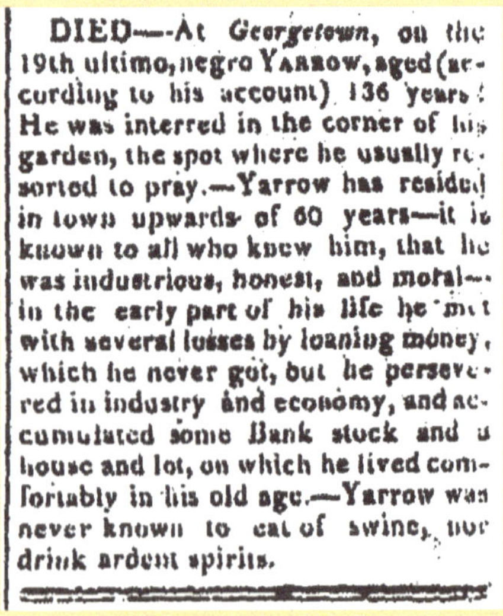

DIED—At *Georgetown*, on the 19th ultimo, negro YARROW, aged (according to his account) 136 years! He was interred in the corner of his garden, the spot where he usually resorted to pray.—Yarrow has resided in town upwards of 60 years—it is known to all who knew him, that he was industrious, honest, and moral—in the early part of his life he met with several losses by loaning money, which he never got, but he persevered in industry and economy, and accumulated some Bank stock and a house and lot, on which he lived comfortably in his old age.—Yarrow was never known to eat of swine, nor drink ardent spirits.

Yarrow Mamout died in Georgetown, 136 years old

However it was not sunshine the whole time around as many politicians were not pleased with the religious neutrality of the Constitution. This often bled into their work as many Americans in 1788 had inaccurate and contradicting views of the Muslim world. Thanks to pressure from the society and politicians, many became pseudo converts (taqiyah) to protect themselves and their families. One such taqiyah is Lamine Kebe who converted to Christianity, to secure a safe passage to Africa. Conversely, slaves like Ayuba Suleiman Diallo refused to change and in his case, his owner was impressed by the fortitude, so much so that the owner freed Ayuba and provided passage back to Africa.

There are two known portraits of Yarrow Mamout, painted by James Alexander Simpson and Charles Wilson Peale

Muslims in the Civil war

There are records indicating two hundred and ninety two Muslims participated during the Civil War in America. Some of the notable people were Private Mohammad Khan, native to Persia but was raised in Afghanistan and emigrated to the United States. Among the 292 soldiers, Captain Moses Osman of the Union army was the highest ranking Muslim officer.

Grave of Captain Moses Osman

Nicholas Said was a former slave to an Arab master but came to the United States in 1860, becoming a teacher in Detroit. Said would later enlist in the 55th Massachusetts Colored Regiment of the United States Army and rose to the rank of Sergeant. Nicholas then transferred to a military hospital, where he gained knowledge of medicine. His army records show that he died in Brownsville. Tennessee in 1882. Another well known Muslim named Hajj Ali, was hired by the U.S Cavalry in 1856 to tend to camels in Arizona and California. Hajj was often playfully referred to as Hi Jolly by his officers and peers and would later become a prospector in Arizona.

Hajj Ali grave in Quartzite, Arizona

Hajj Ali and Gertrudis Sema

Leaders like President George Washington would later maintain several correspondences with the ruler of Morocco Mohammed ben (Bilali) Abdallah in 1777. Bilali Muhammad was a Fula Muslim from Timbo, (present day Guniea-Conarky). He was later enslaved then became the religious leader and Imam for a slave community. During the war of 1812 he and his community protected their master's property from a British attack. Bilali in 1829 authored a 13 page document in Arabic on Islamic beliefs titled 'The Bilali Document.' This document is currently housed at the University of Georgia in Athens.

The Bilali Document is believed to be the first book on Islamic Jurisprudence written in the United States.

A significant event also occurred during the 17th century, before the Civil War; was how the people of the burgeoning country viewed Islam as a religion. This was most evident during the drafting of Pennsylvania's Constitution in 1776. The constitutionalists promoted religious tolerance while the other side called for a reliance on Protestant values. The former group won in the end and added a clause for religious liberty in the State Constitution.

The drafting of the Constitution of Pennsylvania was the first step of many that granted religious freedom to African slaves in America.

Traces of Islamic influence can still be seen in America today, even though the religion underwent a period of silence. For example, the Ring Shout (a type of religious dance) was taught by Muslims like Bilali Mohammed and Salih Bilali in the Georgia Sea Islands. Some interview records from the 1930s contain stories about saraka or rice cakes that were handed out during rituals and feast days. Early blues singers also employed singing styles similar to that of the Adhan or call to prayer.

Enslaved West-African Muslims eating Saraka

Later Years

1840 CE

Later, the U.S saw small scale migration by Muslims in 1840 and this lasted until World War I. Most immigrants came from Yemen and Turkey with the purpose of making good money before moving back to their homeland. Their plans however, would not bear fruit as the economic crisis of 19th century America, kept them from prospering. As a result, the immigrants permanently settled in the United States.

1893 CE

There are many historians that believe Alexander Russell Webb is the earliest prominent Anglo-American to have converted to Islam in 1893. Because of this, he was the sole representative of Islam at the first Parliament of the World's Religions.

World's first religious Parliament

Mohammed Alexander Russell Webb

1900 CE

In 1900, Muslims who lived in Ross, North Dakota had gathered in homes for the first recorded communal prayer held by American Muslims. Ross also had a Muslim cemetery but it was abandoned and torn down during the 1970s.

The tiny brick Mosque in Ross, North Dakota is a reminder of the Mosque erected in 1929.

1906 CE

In 1906 Bosniaks (Muslims living in Bosnia) in Chicago, Illinois started the Dzemijetul Hajrije or the Benevolent Society to help Bosnian Muslims. This is history's longest lasting Muslim community in the United States. They met in Bosnian coffee houses before opening the first Islamic Sunday school. The curriculum and textbooks at the school were written by Bosnian scholar, Sheikh Camil Avdic.

The very next year, Lipka Tatar immigrants from the Podlasie region of Poland founded the first Muslim organization in New York City called the American Mohammedan Society.

Sheikh Camil Avdic

1915 CE

Albanian Muslims constructed a Mosque in Biddeford, Maine. They later established an Islamic Association. Later, in 1919 they built another Mosque in Waterbury, Connecticut. This was one of the first Islamic Associations formed in America.

1921 CE

In Cedar Rapids, Iowa lies the oldest, still standing building that was built mainly to be a Mosque. This Mosque is a tribute to Abdullah Ingram, a notable Muslim veteran who taught the Quran to others. He later wrote a letter to President Eisenhower, asking him to add the M option (for Muslims) on military dog tags.

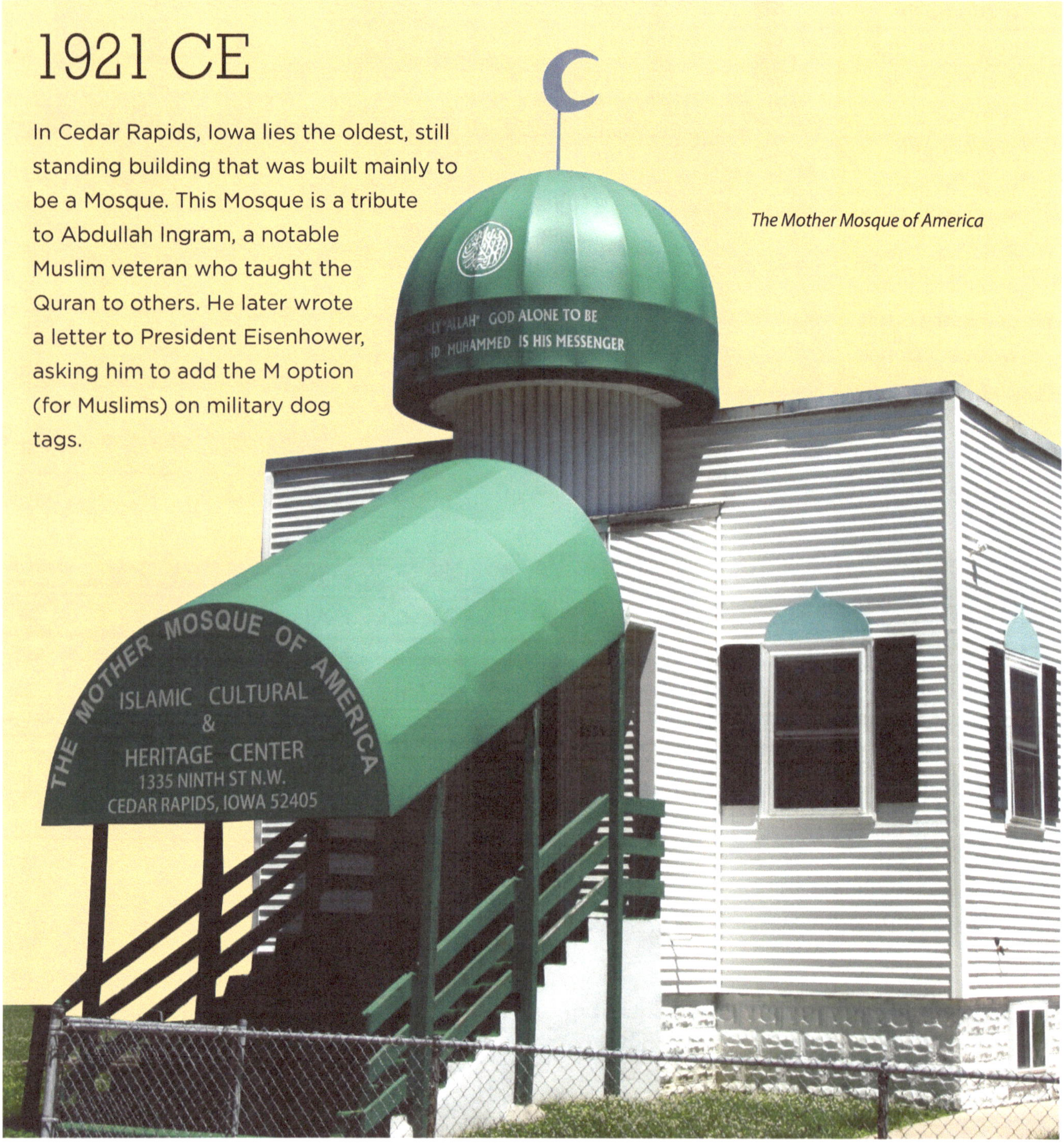

The Mother Mosque of America

A branch of the Ahmadiyya movement was formed in Chicago, Illinois by Dr. Mufti Muhammad Sadiq in the same year. The movement was able to lead many African Americans to the sectarian form of Islam; that is until the NOI began to exert a greater influence.

First missionary of the Ahamadiyya Muslim Community in the United States, Dr. Mufti Muhammad

The al-Sadiq Center is one of America's earliest and oldest standing centers in America today.

1922 CE

Tatar Muslims who came from Poland, formed a congregation in 1917. The group was led by Sam Rafelowich, the son of a Polish Imam. During 1922 the community established a mosque in Brooklyn that is still in use today.

1947 CE

The oldest known mosque in the West Coast is the Muslim Mosque of Sacramento. This was constructed by Muslims from India in 1947. Many immigrant Muslims arrived via ship to the port cities of San Francisco and Vancouver in the early 1900s and migrated to Sacramento Valley, to search for better farming opportunities. The mosque today is one of the few thriving mosques in the city, with a diverse membership.

Muslim Mosque of Sacramento

1948 CE

The Ahmadiyya Movement in Islam brought together delegates from mission centers in Cleveland, Kansas City, Washington D.C., Chicago and Pittsburgh. Those from smaller communities opted to elect national secretaries to represent them. The movement set up educational and social work programs in order to propagate their faith. Construction of the mosques sped up between 1920 and 1930. By 1952, there were more than twenty mosques in the country with California having more mosques than any other state.

American Fazl Mosque, Washington DC

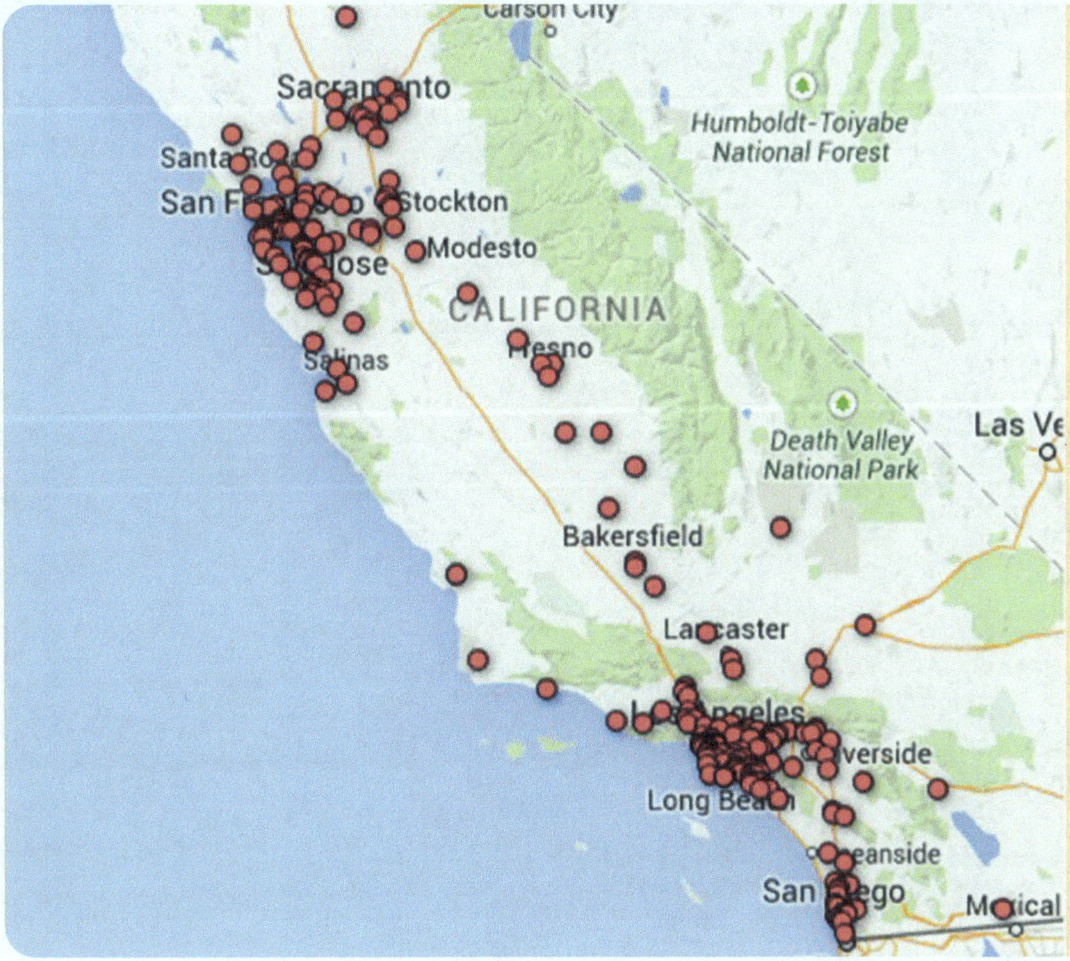

Mosques in California as of 2014

1952 CE

Muslims then held the first National Muslim conference at Cedar Rapids, Iowa. A total of four hundred Muslims from all over North America attended the conference. This event laid down the groundwork for the Federation of Islamic Associations of the United States and Canada or FIA that was founded on July of next year. The Federation's leaders were all American-born.

Sheikh Dawood Ahmed Faisal

1955 CE

In 1955, Sheikh Dawood Ahmed Faisal constructed a State Street Masjid in New York City. This was done to help the African-American Muslim Community.

1957 CE

Washington D. C's Islamic Centre was conceptualized and constructed by Abraham Joseph Essa Howar. Abraham Howar was an immigrant from Jerusalem who also played a great role in the local diplomatic community. There were many Muslim countries that also contributed to the effort. President Dwight D. Eisenhower dedicated the center, citing that the United States has enjoyed the multitude of Muslim contributions to American Society.

Islamic Centre of Washington

1962 CE

The case of Fulwood V. Clemmer about the religious services for Muslims in prison was an important moment in the Evolution of Islam. The U.S. District Court for the District of Columbia decided that Islam would qualify for protection. This is because the court found that Islam fit the definition of religion as 'theistic' and of 'ultimate concern' to the believer's life. Because of this decision, the court would order prison to provide facilities for religious services to Muslims as they did for Jewish, Protestant and Catholic inmates.

1963 CE

Many of the African-American converts to Islam would seek to create an alternative Islamic community in New Your City for them to call their own. This attempt was started in 1963 but was broken apart after 1965. African-American Muslims in 1967 broke away from the State Street Mosque to form their own center in Brooklyn, led by Imam Yahya Abdul-Kareem. The group would later clash with FBI officials over the desecration of their mosque, followed by the brotherhood committing themselves to building a National Dar Ul-Islam Federation of Sunni Muslim family communities.

Also In 1963, the Shia community of Dearborn built the first Shia mosque in North America, located on Joy Road in Detroit. This was done through the efforts of Imam Mohammad Jawad Chirri, who obtained funds from the then President of Egypt, Jamal Abdul Nasser.

In the 1980s the Dearborn Mosque obtained a permit to broadcast the call to prayer using loudspeakers. It was the first mosque in America to do so.

There is an estimate of nearly 786,000 Shia Muslims living in the United States. These Muslims originate from South Asia, Europe, Middle East and East Africa. The heart of 'Shiism' is located in Dearborn U.S., which is also home to the Islamic Centre of America. Then there's the North American Shia Ithna Asheri Muslim Communities Organization or NASIMCO, which is the largest umbrella group for North American Shias.

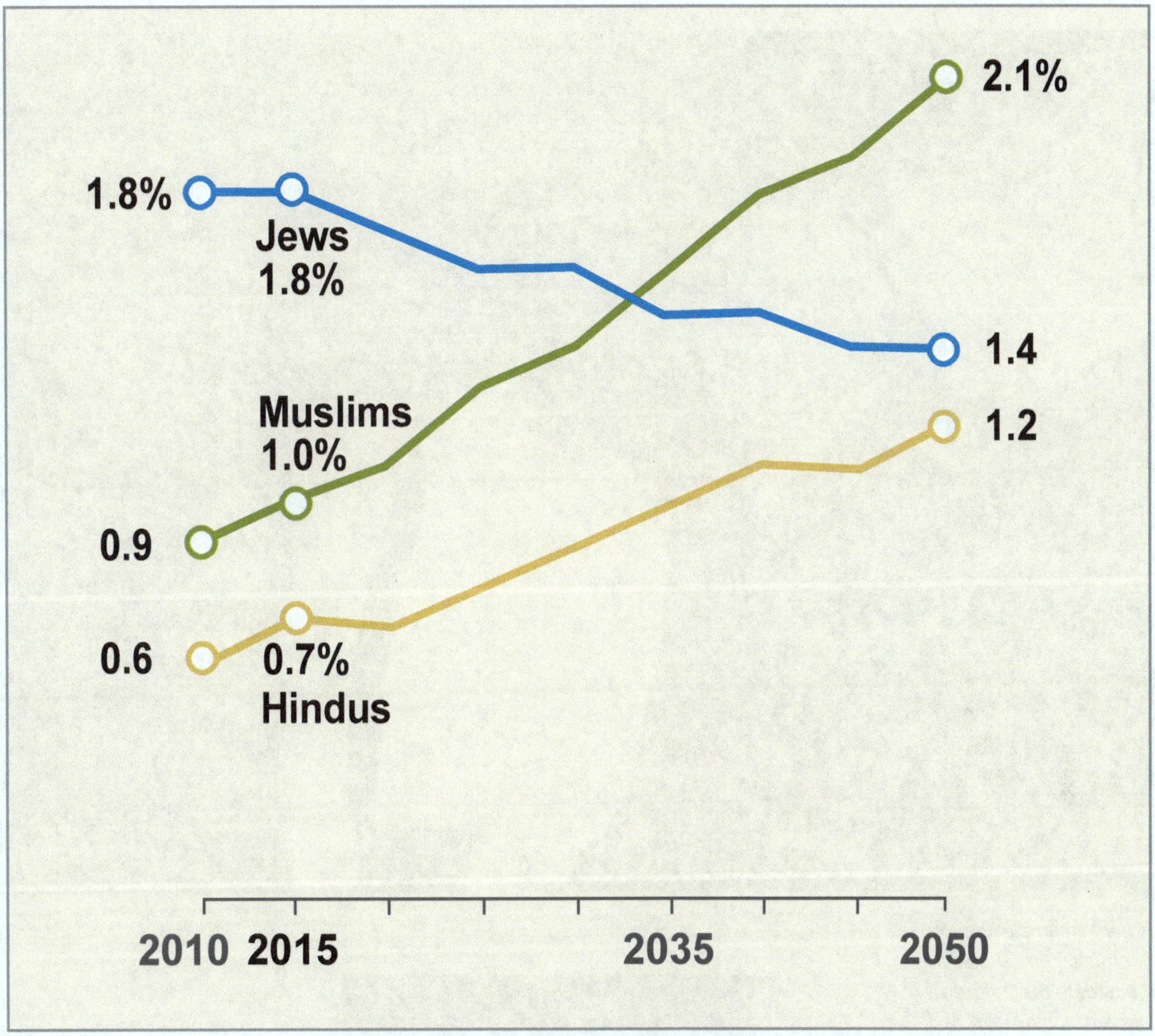

2015 Survey taken by The Future of World Religions: Population Growth Projections

1965 CE

During 1965, Congress passed the Immigration and Nationality Act; that ended the quota system put in place in 1924. This act halted the immigration from Asia to the United States for more than 40 years. It also placed a significant limitation on immigrants from non-European countries. Because of this, a number of immigrants settled in America, many of which were Muslims.

1991 CE

The Muslim Members of the Military (MMM) held the first "Unity in Uniform" conference, meant to address the absence of Muslim chaplains in the armed services. At present, there are over 5,000 Muslims on active duty in the United States Military.

Chaplain Arnold Resnicoff attaches new shoulder boards to the uniform of Imam Monja Malak Abd al-Muta Noel Jr, 1996.

Charles Bilal

Also in Texas, Charles Bilal became the first Muslim Mayor in the United States when he got the position to govern the town of Kountze, Texas.

2006 CE

Keith Ellison from Minnesota was the first Muslim who was elected to Congress. He was sworn into the U.S House of Representatives using the Quran that Thomas Jefferson owned. Ellison was also re-elected in 2010.

Keith Ellison

2008 CE

In Berkley, California; Zaytuna College opened its doors to encourage a deeper engagement between Muslims and scholars of Islam and a traditional liberal arts education. Under the motto of 'Where Islam meets America', the school followed a precedent already set forward by Christian and Jewish colleges to foster a multidisciplinary approach to education. They also aimed to maintain a discourse rooted in religious tradition.

Did you know

Zaytuna College was the first Muslim Liberal Arts college in the United States

Zaytuna College Campus

Today's Muslims

Despite the inclusion of Keith Ellison, the first Muslim elected to the U.S Congress in 2007, the integration of Muslim Americans into the American political system has been met with negativity. Rep. Ellison is constantly under fire from colleagues and pundits to prove his loyalty to his country. The U.S census does not collect information on a person's religious affiliation, there is no official statistics on the number of Muslims in the United States. The Pew Research Centre in 2011 conducted a survey and found that there were about 1.8 million Muslim adults (2.75 million are from all ages) in the U.S. The Council on American-Islamic Relations or CAIR which is a Washington based advocacy group puts the number at much higher, estimating the number ranges between 6-7 million. Regardless of their true numbers and their long history as part of the American society dating back to the founding of the country, many Muslim Americans are being treated as unwelcome foreigners.

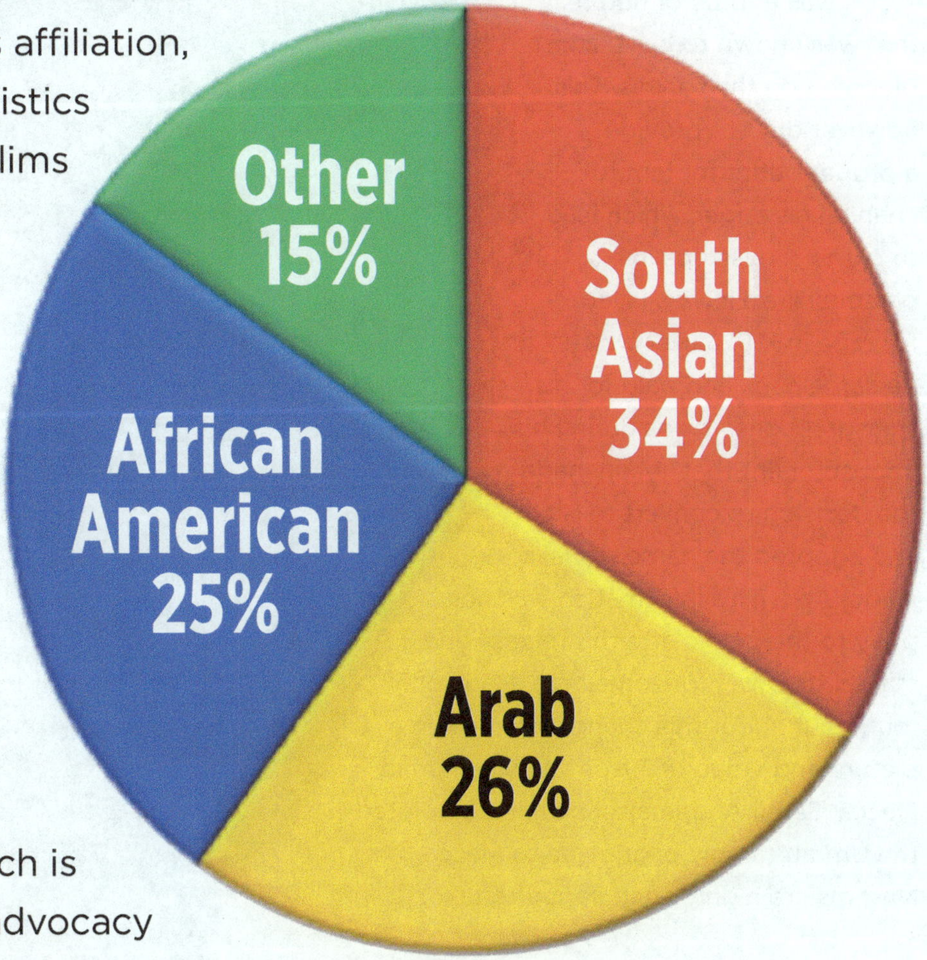

Celebrities who converted to Islam

Among those who have converted to Islam, there are a notable number of celebrities who have also changed their faith. Some of them are:

Mike Tyson

To the many that did not see his career from the 1980's to the early 1990's, Mike Tyson was the most feared boxer on the planet. Tyson was a force of nature that was known to leave men bloodied on the canvas. This however did not provide a proper outlet for him to channel his anger, which lead to criminal missteps in his personal life. He was jailed for rape in 1992, after which he came back and paid for his transgressions. It was during his imprisonment that Tyson made the decision to convert to Islam and adopted the name of Malik Abdul Aziz. This information was not privy to the public after his release and stayed that way for some time. Many only found out about this change later, when a picture and video of Tyson showing him in Mecca, Saudi Arabia after he had completed the Umrah (a holy pilgrimage to Mecca that Muslims are highly encouraged to take).

Did you know

Mike Tyson was the first heavyweight boxer to hold the WBA, WBC and IBF titles at the same time.

Muhammad Ali

Born Cassius Clay Jr. later known as Muhammad Ali, Cassius Clay Jr's public conversion to Islam was one that defined his life while also being one that enraged his critics. There were also the people in his hometown newspaper that continued to refer to him as Cassius for years. Ali's embrace of Islam also led to his refusal to participate in the Vietnam war, a decision that cost him his title, his livelihood and cemented his status in American history.

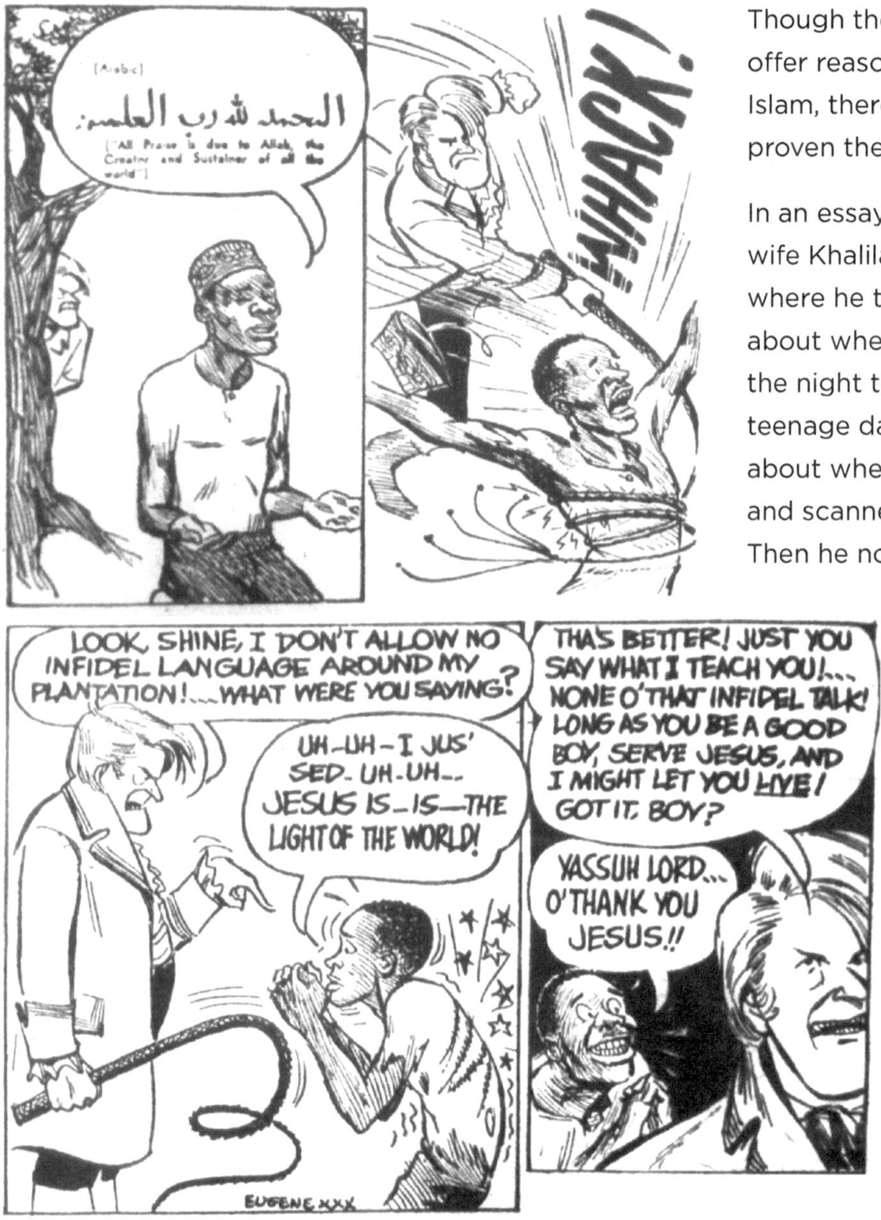

Comic that made Cassius Clay Jr. convert to Islam

Though there are numerous stories that offer reasons why he chose to embrace Islam, there is an article in TIME that has proven the most definitive of all.

In an essay that he wrote to his second wife Khalilah Camacho Ali, during a period where he thought himself a God, Ali wrote about when he was Cassius Clay Jr. and the night that his life changed. During his teenage days in Louisville, Cassius spoke about when he left the roller skating rink and scanned the sidewalk for pretty girls. Then he noticed a man in a black mohair suit that sold newspapers for the Nation of Islam. Though he knew of the leader Elijah Muhammad, Cassius did not give any serious thought to joining the group that was known for using elements of Islam to preach black separatism and self improvement. Nevertheless, Cassius politely took the newspaper and noticed a cartoon about a slave owner beating his black slave and insisting that the man pray to Jesus. Ali wrote in the letter that it did something to him and it made sense. It made him realize that he did not choose his religion nor his name itself and since that was the case, he did not need to keep those forms of slavery on him. That comic was the humble beginning that led to the biggest change in Ali's life.

Did you know

Before NOI leader Elijah Muhammad, gave Cassius Clay Jr. his new name, he called himself Cassius X for a short time, renouncing his slave name.

Malcolm X

Born Malcolm Little on May 19, 1925, Little would grow up to become an American leader and he passed away on February 21, 1965. Malcolm X had a turbulent childhood when he lost his father at age 6 while his mother was forced into an asylum when he turned 13. Thanks to this, he was forced to live in several foster homes and would later be caught for breaking and entering at age 20. It was his time spent in prison that helped shape him and aid in his joining in the Nation of Islam. After obtaining his parole in 1952, Malcolm X would become the organization's most influential leaders.

Later becoming disillusioned with the NOI's views, Malcolm X left the organization. He then travelled across Africa and Middle East to perform the Hajj. Malcolm cited on many occasions that one of the reasons he converted to Islam was because of how he was accepted by those already following Islam. The religion allowed him to freely express himself. Another reason for his conversion was of the neutrality that the religion had. During his trip to Mecca, he visited many of the Muslims in their world and enjoyed the reception and recognition that came with being a brother in religion.

Malcolm X rose the ranks in the NOI, thanks in whole to his charismatic speeches

Did you know

Although Malcolm X and Martin Luther King Jr. were both major figures in the Civil Rights Movement, they met only once.

Kareem Abdul-Jabbar

Born Ferdinand Lewis Alcindor Jr, Kareem Abdul-Jabbar is a retired American Basketball player who has played 20 seasons in the NBA for the LA Lakers and Mulwaukee Bucks in the center position. Abdul-Jabbar holds many records in NBA, ranging from MVP to NBA All-Star with NBA coach Pat Riley and players like Julius Erving and Isiah Thomas calling him the greatest basketball player of all time.

Kareem Abdul Jabbar has cited the autobiography of Malcolm X inspired him to convert to Islam

It was in the summer of 1968 that Alcindor participated in the Shahada (Islamic creed declaring belief in the oneness of God and acceptance of Muhammad as God's Prophet) then converted to Sunni Islam. Though he had converted, he did not publicly use his new Arabic name till 1971. He also boycotted the 1968 Summer Olympics by not trying out for the U.S Men's Olympic Basketball team in a protest to the unequal treatment of African-Americans in the United States.

Did you know

Kareem Abdul Jabbar's famous sky hook was developed due to a ban on dunking imposed in 1965.

Islamic Architecture in U.S.A

The growth of Islam in America has also seen the rise of numerous Mosques constructed to accommodate the people. As of a 2010 survey, the number of mosques in the country was approximately 2,106 but that number continues to rise in conjunction with the Muslim population. Among these mosques are some noted for their beautiful architecture and vibrant design. They are:

Dar al-Islam Mosque- Abiquiu, New Mexico

Located in Abiquiu, an hour north of Santa Fe, Mexico lies the architecturally unique Dar al-Islam Mosque. Egyptian architect Hassan Fathy built the mosque using mud bricks (adobe).

The main buildings were completed in 1981 and officially opened in 1982. The Mosque offers religious instruction, workshops on Islam and recently added a number of residential units, able to accommodate 150 people.

Exterior of the mosque

Diyanet Center of America - Lanham, Maryland

Located in the Washington Metropolitan Area lies the DCA or Diyanet Center of America; a non-profit organization serving the needs of the Muslims in the immediate area. The complex was built in 1993 by the Turkish American Islamic Foundation, later changed to Turkish American Community Center. Since its completion, the Center has received major support from the Presidency of Religious Affairs of the Government of Turkey. The Center is made up of five main buildings, all constructed in the classical Ottoman style of architecture. The Center also has other buildings like a guest house, a cultural center building and a recreational building. This building also has a Turkish bath, an indoor pool and a sports center.

The interior of the Diyanet Center

Islamic Center of Washington-Washington, D.C

The idea for this Islamic Center was conceived in 1944, after the Turkish ambassador died and there was no mosque to hold his funeral in. The site to construct the mosque was purchased in 1946 and the cornerstone was laid in 1949. Through the combined effort of the Washington diplomatic community, the Muslim American community and the Islamic Nations of the world, the Islamic Center was completed by 1957. Since it's completion, the Islamic Center has been visited by a number of high profile dignitaries and several Presidents.

Former President George W. Bush visiting the Islamic Center on September 17, 2001

Noor Islamic Cultural Center-Columbus, Ohio

The Noor Islamic Cultural Center or NICC is a mosque and cultural center in Columbus, Ohio, USA. Construction started in 2001 and was finished five years after. The NICC was the first Islamic center used as a polling place in Central Ohio. The Mosque sits on a wide lawn with ponds on one side and a parking lot on the other. There are two domes at each end of the center. The exterior walls are stucco with no minarets. The center's unique look reflects an amalgamation of American and Islamic architecture that fits well with its surroundings.

The Noor Islamic Cultural Center is the largest mosque in Columbus

Islamic Center of America- Dearborn, Michigan

The Islamic Center of America is widely regarded as one of the oldest Islamic institutions in the United States, dating back to as early as 1940. The building consists of a large domed prayer hall, a kitchen, a lecture hall, two classrooms and an office. When construction for the center was completed in 1963, it saw an influx of families move in to the area. As a result, by 1967, the center had outgrown its space and additional classrooms, a social hall and a minaret were added.

Exterior of the Mosque